MY PET

Hamsters & Gerbils

Honor Head

Photographs by
Jane Burton

RAINTREE
STECK-VAUGHN
RSVP PUBLISHERS

A Harcourt Company
Austin New York
www.steck-vaughn.com

Published by Raintree Steck-Vaughn Publishers, an imprint of Steck-Vaughn Company.

Editors: Claire Edwards, Erik Greb
Art Director: Max Brinkmann
Designer: Rosamund Saunders
Illustrator: Pauline Bayne

Printed in Singapore

1 2 3 4 5 6 7 8 9 0 LB 03 02 01 00

Library of Congress Cataloging-in-Publication Data

Head, Honor.
  Hamsters & gerbils/Honor Head; photographs by Jane Burton.
    p. cm.—(My pet)
  Summary: Describes the physical characteristics and habits of hamsters and gerbils and tells how to care for them as pets.
  ISBN 0-7398-2886-X (hardcover)
  ISBN 0-7398-3010-4 (softcover)
  1. Hamsters as pets—Juvenile literature.
  2. Gerbils as pets—Juvenile literature.
  [1. Hamsters as pets. 2. Gerbils as pets.
  3. Pets.] I. Title: Hamsters and gerbils.
  II. Burton, Jane, ill. III. Title.
SF459.H3 H33 2000
636.9'356—dc21
                            00–027048

Contents

My Hamster

whiskers

ears

front paws

claws

tail

My Gerbil

ears

tail

whiskers

claws

4

It's fun to have your own pet.

Hamsters and gerbils are fun to have as pets, but they are small and easily frightened. You should treat them gently and look after them carefully.

Hamsters and gerbils need to be fed every day. You will also have to keep their homes clean and make sure they are happy and healthy.

Young children with pets should always work with an adult. For further notes, please see page 32.

What is a gerbil?

A gerbil is a little animal
that looks like a mouse.
It has strong back legs,
long feet, little front paws,
and a long tail.

**Gerbils are very lively
and curious. They
like to explore and
scurry around.**

Most gerbils are brown, but some are gray, white, gold, or black. Some have stripes or patches.

Gerbils like to live in groups. Never keep one gerbil by itself.

What is a hamster?

A hamster is a little bigger than a gerbil. It has a small, stumpy tail. Hamsters sleep for most of the day. Then, they wake up and play in the evening.

There are lots of different types of hamsters.

In the wild, hamsters live in deserts. They sleep in tunnels under the ground.

8

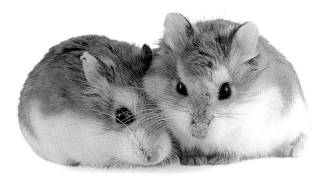

Some hamsters are very small. Some hamsters have stripes or patterns on their fur.

Some hamsters have long hair. They look cuddly, but they need to be brushed a lot.

Gerbils and hamsters make nests for their young.

When a gerbil or hamster is pregnant, the mother makes a nest out of hay, straw, or special paper bedding from a pet store.

Gerbils and hamsters are
born with no fur and with their
eyes closed. Young gerbils and
hamsters drink their mother's
milk. This is called suckling.

**When a mother is
feeding her babies,
she needs lots of
water, fresh milk
every day, and extra
food, such as cheese or egg.**

Hamsters and gerbils are
ready to leave their mother
at about six
weeks old.

Your pet will need a place to live.

Hamsters and gerbils can live in a cage or a tank. This hamster tank has a nest box on top. The cage below has two nest boxes. It has a clear lid that fits on top to keep the animals from escaping.

Put a deep layer of wood shavings in the tank or cage for your pet to chew and dig in.

Your pet will need some nesting material. Put in some hay or paper bedding from the pet store.

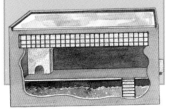

You may buy or make your pet a cage. Make sure that the cage does not have any sharp edges.

Give your pet some toys to play with.

Hamsters and gerbils will enjoy playing with toys such as this tube. Never give them metal toys or anything painted.

If you let your pet out of its cage, so it can run free, shut all windows and doors. Watch your pet all the time—hamsters and gerbils are very small and very fast.

You can buy toys from a pet store, or make them. Keep toilet rolls or half of a coconut shell for your pet to explore.

Gerbils like to dig underground. Make a hill of wood shavings, so that your pet can burrow into it.

Give your hamster an exercise wheel. Make sure there are no gaps in it, or the hamster's feet might get caught. Gerbils do not need a wheel—they prefer to burrow.

You will need to take care of your pet.

Give your pet a piece of hard wood, a special gnawing block, or a Brazil nut in its shell to chew on. This will help to keep its teeth sharp and short.

This gerbil is listening for danger noises. Gerbils and hamsters have very good hearing and do not like loud noises. Do not keep them near a television or a stereo speaker.

If your hamster is asleep, don't wake it up. It needs to sleep during the day.

Never use cotton, knitting wool, or pieces of clothing for bedding. Your pet may try to eat the material, or it may get its legs tangled in it. Never use newspaper, because the ink will harm your pet.

Your pet will need fresh food every day.

Give your pet special hamster and gerbil food in the evening. Clean out any old food. Do not give your pet too much food, because it will go bad.

Put the food in a heavy dish, so that your pet cannot knock it over.

Give your pet some fresh fruit or vegetables every morning. It will enjoy carrots, apples, pears, grapes, and tomatoes. Do not give it lettuce. Remember to wash all fresh food.

Make sure your pet
has fresh water every
day. Put the water in
a special drip feeder
rather than a bowl.

Hamsters carry food
around in their cheek
pouches. They also
like to store food
in their bedding.

You will need to keep your pet's home clean.

Remove old food from your pet's cage or tank once a day. You will also need to remove droppings from your hamster's cage every day.

Clean your pet's home once a week. Take out the floor covering and put in a fresh layer.

When you clean your pet's home, wear gloves, or wash your hands with soap and warm water afterward.

Once a week put in some new nesting material for your pet, but do not throw out the old nest.

Once a month give your hamster's home a good cleaning. Your gerbils will need this only every three months.

Wash the cage or tank with soapy water and special pet spray to kill germs. Make sure it is dry before you put in new floor and nesting material.

Be gentle with your pet.

Your pet will be frightened when you first pick it up. Move slowly, and do not reach down from above. Offer your pet a piece of food and talk to it quietly.

Do not squeeze your pet or hold it by its tail. Stroke it gently from neck to tail.

When you are holding your pet, sit or kneel, or hold it on a table. If your pet does fall and you think it is hurt, take it to a vet right away.

Be careful if you hold your finger out to a hamster. It may think it is food—and bite!

When your pet is tame, it will enjoy running from one hand to another. It may run onto your shoulder and up and down your arm.

Help your pet stay healthy.

Hamsters and gerbils groom themselves
to keep their fur clean and shiny.
If your pet's fur looks dull, or if your
pet has runny eyes or a runny nose, you
may need to take it to the vet.

If you feed your pet well and keep its home clean, your pet should stay healthy. A healthy animal has bright eyes, a smooth coat, and a clean nose, bottom, and ears.

Your pet needs lots of things to gnaw on. If its teeth grow too long, it may not be able to eat properly. If this happens, take it to the vet, who will file your pet's teeth for you.

Your pet may become sick if its cage is in a draft, or if it is kept too near a radiator or in direct sunlight.

Hamsters like to live alone, but gerbils like to live in groups.

Gerbils and hamsters should not be kept together, since they will fight. Hamsters also fight each other, so it is better to keep one hamster by itself.

If a hamster has toys, and you play with it every day, it won't get lonely.

Gerbils live in groups in the wild, so one gerbil on its own will be lonely.

Always keep two gerbils together. Make sure they are females from the same litter, so that they are happy together and do not have babies.

Gerbils enjoy living in a tank filled with a mixture of moss, earth, and chopped straw. They can burrow into the earth.

Your pet may live for several years.

Hamsters and gerbils may live for up to three years. As your pet gets older, it might lose its fur and put on weight. Make sure you do not feed it too much.

If your pet escapes from its cage, do not chase it. Close all windows and doors. Put out some food and wait. Your pet will come out to eat, and then you can scoop it up gently.

If you look after your pet carefully and treat it gently, it will have a happy life. But just like people, one day it will die.

You may feel sad when your pet dies, but you will be able to remember how much fun you had together.

Words to Remember

bedding Soft straw, hay, or special paper for an animal to sleep in. Also called nesting material.

burrow To dig underground.

desert Land where there is almost no rain.

gnaw To chew something with the front teeth.

groom To brush an animal. Animals groom themselves with their paws.

pouches Spaces in a hamster's cheeks where it can store food.

scurry To move around quickly.

suckling When a hamster or gerbil drinks its mother's milk, it is suckling.

vet An animal doctor.

whiskers Long fine hairs that grow on an animal's face.

Hamsters and Gerbils Grow Fast

A gerbil at one day old.

A gerbil at one week old.

Gerbils at five weeks old.

A hamster at three days old, suckling.

Hamsters at 14 days old.

Index

Notes for Parents

Hamsters and gerbils will give you and your family a great deal of pleasure, but owning any pet is a responsibility. If you decide to buy a pet for your child, you will need to ensure that the animal is healthy and happy. You will also have to care for it if it is ill, and help your child care for the animal until he or she is at least seven years old. It will be your responsibility to make sure your child does not harm the gerbils or hamster, and learns to handle them correctly.

Here are some other points to think about before you decide to own hamsters or gerbils.

- Hamsters and gerbils should be six weeks old before leaving their mothers.

- Hamsters sleep during most of the day and should not be disturbed. If this is going to be frustrating for children, gerbils may be a better choice of pet.

- Hamsters and gerbils must not be kept anywhere too hot or too cold. If hamsters become too cold, they may go into hibernation and die.

- You need to have space to keep the gerbils or hamsters indoors. A hamster cage or gerbil tank should measure at least 30 x 15 x 15 inches. A gerbil cage should be at least 25 x 10 x 10 inches, but this varies depending on how many gerbils you keep.

- Do not keep female and male gerbils together. Hamsters should be kept on their own.

- When you go on vacation, you will need to make sure someone can care for your pets while you are away.

- If you have cats or dogs, keep them away from hamsters and gerbils. These little animals are easily upset and can become ill from shock.

This book is only an introduction for young readers. If you have any questions about how to look after your pet, you can contact the Humane Society of the U.S., 2100 L Street NW, Washington, DC 20037.